## A NOTE TO PARENTS

When your children are ready to "step into reading," giving them the right books is as crucial as giving them the right food to eat. **Step into Reading Books** present exciting stories and information reinforced with lively, colorful illustrations that make learning to read fun, satisfying, and worthwhile. They are priced so that acquiring an entire library of them is affordable. And they are beginning readers with a difference—they're written on five levels.

**Early Step into Reading Books** are designed for brand-new readers, with large type and only one or two lines of very simple text per page. **Step 1 Books** feature the same easy-to-read type as the Early Step into Reading Books, but with more words per page. **Step 2 Books** are both longer and slightly more difficult, while **Step 3 Books** introduce readers to paragraphs and fully developed plot lines. **Step 4 Books** offer exciting nonfiction for the increasingly independent reader.

The grade levels assigned to the five steps—preschool through kindergarten for the Early Books, preschool through grade 1 for Step 1, grades 1 through 3 for Step 2, grades 2 through 3 for Step 3, and grades 2 through 4 for Step 4—are intended only as guides. Some children move through all five steps very rapidly; others climb the steps over a period of several years. Either way, these books will help your child "step into reading" in style!

The editors would like to thank Dr. Thomas R. Holtz, Jr. and Dr. Michael Brett-Surman for their invaluable contribution to the preparation of this book.

Illustrations copyright © 2001 by Michael Skrepnick.

Illustrations of Charles Darwin and Thomas Huxley are based on photographs from the Culver Pictures collection.

*Library of Congress Cataloging-in-Publication Data*
Shealy, Dennis R. Dinosaurs alive! / the dinosaur-bird connection / by Dennis R. Shealy ; illustrated by Michael Skrepnick.
   p. cm. — (Step into reading)
SUMMARY: Discusses the evolutionary link between dinosaurs and birds.
ISBN 0-375-81296-2 (pbk.) — ISBN 0-375-91296-7 (lib. bdg.)
1. Dinosaurs—Juvenile literature. 2. Birds—Evolution—Juvenile literature. [1. Dinosaurs. 2. Birds. 3. Evolution.]
I. Skrepnick, Michael William, ill. II. Title. III. Series. QE861.5 .S48 2001 567.9—dc21
2001041757

www.randomhouse.com/kids

www.jpinstitute.com

Printed in the United States of America
First Edition November 2001  10 9 8 7 6 5 4 3 2 1

*On the cover: Little* Sinosauropteryx *stalking through the forests of China 125 million years ago. Fossils of* Sinosauropteryx *were the first proof that many groups of dinosaurs had a covering of feathers.*

Step into Reading®

JURASSIC PARK™ INSTITUTE

Dinosaurs Alive!

The Dinosaur-Bird Connection

by
Dennis R. Shealy

illustrated by
Michael Skrepnick

A Step 4 Book

Random House 🏠 New York

# Chapter 1
# They're Alive!

Take a walk outside and chances are you will see a dinosaur. Yes, a *living* dinosaur. They are everywhere—in the sky, in trees, even sitting on telephone wires. If you are lucky, you may even get one to eat out of your hand.

Happily, there is little chance these dinosaurs will bite your hand. Most, in fact, would fit *in* it. That's because these dinosaurs are birds. All kinds of birds. Birds are living dinosaurs.

*You're kidding, right?*
No, I am not kidding. To explain, we need to go back to the Age of Dinosaurs. Let's start there.

It is 70 million years ago. *Tyrannosaurus* (tie-RAN-uh-SAW-rus) is the top **predator**. It is as long and heavy as a school bus. *Tyrannosaurus* stands on two legs and can run fast. Its huge mouth is filled with long, sharp teeth, made for eating meat.

*Tyrannosaurus* belongs to a group of dinosaurs called **theropods**. Theropods are known for their large size. But there were also some much smaller theropods. The best-known of them are probably *Velociraptor* (vuh-LAHS-uh-RAP-tur) and *Deinonychus* (die-NON-ih-kus). (You may remember the scary "raptors" from the *Jurassic Park* movies.) **Raptors** like *Velociraptor* and *Deinonychus* were excellent hunters. They were fast and alert. They had to be. Being quick helped them catch **prey**. It also kept them from *becoming* prey!

Velociraptor *was a swift runner. A stiff tail allowed it to make quick, sharp turns while chasing prey.*

Raptors were different from their larger theropod cousins in another important way. They had long arms with long hands and fingers. Big theropods, like *Tyrannosaurus,* had short arms with small hands. These features were not very useful. But the raptors' long arms and hands were *very* useful. They could use them to grasp at and hold on to prey.

Long arms helped raptors in another way, too. They improved the raptors' balance, which helped them to run faster.

Being able to grasp and run fast were useful **traits**. They helped the raptors stay alive. In fact, many different types of raptors lived for millions of years.

*But wait a minute! What do raptors have to do with . . . roosters or robins?*

To explain, we need to go back even earlier in Earth's history. Several *billion* years earlier.

# Chapter 2
## Evolution and Extinction

The first living things appeared on Earth over three billion years ago. Over millions of years, these simple life forms became more and more complex. Eventually, they became all the plants and animals that now live on Earth. But the fact that a living thing exists today does not mean that it has always existed. Many different groups of living things have died out and no longer exist. They became **extinct**.

Volcanoes, earthquakes, and changing sea levels made Earth a dangerous place to live. However, just as some living things became extinct, others stayed alive. Some were strong enough to prey on other animals. Some were swift enough to escape being eaten. Still others were better at hiding. Animals that stayed alive passed their useful traits to their babies. Those babies were then more likely to grow up and to have babies of their own.

Over millions of years, the kind of **environment** an animal lived in would change. Sometimes the animal's traits would change to help it stay alive. Many small changes could add up, turning the animal into a new and different kind of living thing. This slow process of change is called **evolution**.

Dimetrodon *was a dangerous predator that lived long before the first dinosaur appeared.*

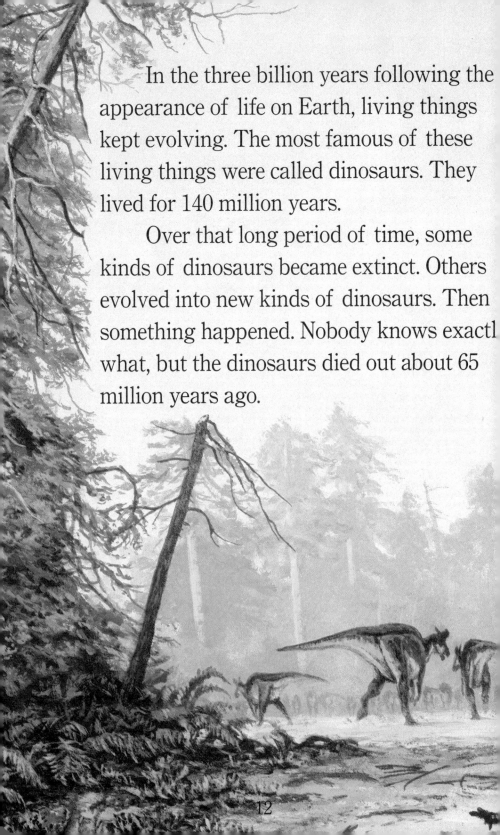

In the three billion years following the appearance of life on Earth, living things kept evolving. The most famous of these living things were called dinosaurs. They lived for 140 million years.

Over that long period of time, some kinds of dinosaurs became extinct. Others evolved into new kinds of dinosaurs. Then something happened. Nobody knows exactl what, but the dinosaurs died out about 65 million years ago.

*They all became, like, extinct. Right?*

That is what people thought for a long time. Today, we know that is not true.

# Chapter 3
## *Archaeopteryx*—A Dinosaur in Bird's Clothing

By the mid-1800s, the "idea" of evolution had been around for over one hundred years. Still, **biologists** (scientists who study living things) had little proof that living things were changing. But **geologists** (scientists who study the Earth) had lots of proof that the planet was changing.

Geologists could point at forces such as moving water and wind that caused Earth's surface to change. They could point at seashells found in the desert to prove that water once covered what is now dry land. But there were no such things for biologists to point at. Because of this, most people believed that living things had never changed. They believed this even though **fossils** existed of animals—such as the dinosaurs—that were no longer alive.

Then in 1859, scientist Charles Darwin published his book *On the Origin of Species*. In it, Darwin said that every living animal was a **descendant** of an animal that had evolved over time. This was not a new idea. But Darwin realized that evolution was simply the result of animals living with each other in their environment. Just trying to stay alive was a force (like running water) that could cause one **species** of animal to change into another. Darwin called this process of change **natural selection**.

*Charles Darwin*

Natural selection took place when an animal with traits useful in its environment stayed alive long enough to have babies. But as geologists knew, a species' environment might change over time. The weather could turn colder. A water source might dry up. Or a new predator could move in. These changes would affect—or, in Darwin's term, "select"—which traits best helped an animal stay alive. Bit by bit, the traits that helped a species stay alive might change so much that it evolved into a *new* species.

*Thomas Huxley was called "Darwin's Bulldog" because of his strong support of the theory of evolution.*

Many people did not agree with Darwin. If he was right, then why weren't there animals walking around that were evolving into new species? Darwin's answer was that evolution takes place over long periods of time. No person could see it happen during his or her life. That answer did not convince everyone. But Darwin's ideas gave biologists a way to start explaining the fossils of extinct species. It now made sense that species of all shapes and sizes could have lived, evolved, and later become extinct.

In 1861—just two years after *On the Origin of Species* was published—the fossil skeleton of a small crow-sized animal was found in Germany. It had teeth and a tail, and some of its bones were like dinosaur bones. It looked just like the fossil skeleton of the small dinosaur *Compsognathus* (KOMP-sog-NAY-thus). But this fossil had a very strange feature—*feathers!* The animal was given the name *Archaeopteryx* (AHR-kee-OP-tuh-riks), which means "ancient wing."

*(Top)* Archaeopteryx;
*(middle)* fossil of
Archaeopteryx; *(bottom)*
Compsognathus

Scientists today know that *Archaeopteryx* shows a "step" in the evolution between dinosaurs and modern birds. But few people saw this in 1861. Darwin's ideas were far from being accepted. Many scientists did not know what to make of the feathered fossil.

**Archaeopteryx** *leaping at a lizard*

But biologist Thomas Huxley had already seen a connection between birds and dinosaurs. About a year before the discovery of the *Archaeopteryx* fossil, he found that the leg bones of the dinosaur *Megalosaurus* (MEG-uh-lo-SAW-rus) had thirty-five things in common with the leg bones of an ostrich. Huxley said that modern birds *must* have evolved from some type of dinosaur—but almost no one believed him!

**Megalosaurus**

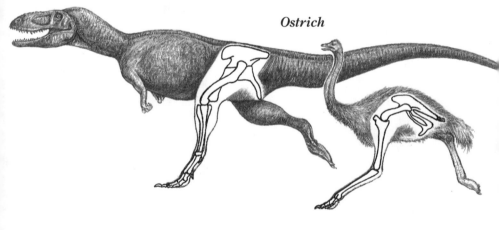

*Ostrich*

Despite the discovery of *Archaeopteryx* and Huxley's work, most scientists did not think of modern birds as the descendants of dinosaurs. They believed that birds and dinosaurs might have shared a relative in the distant past (like cousins), but the idea that birds were direct descendants (like great-grandchildren) of dinosaurs was out of the question!

*So let me get this straight. Just because some old fossil had feathers, I'm supposed to believe that birds evolved from dinosaurs?*

No. There is more proof to come. But you are not alone in questioning this idea. **Paleontologists** (scientists who study the history of life on Earth) argued about it for almost a hundred years. Then a paleontologist in the 1960s made some very important discoveries. People quit asking if dinosaurs and birds *could* be related—and started talking about how closely they *are* related!

# Chapter 4
## A New Look at Old Bones

Biologists study living things and put them into groups. They compare traits, such as backbones and body temperature. They also look at things like whether females lay eggs or give birth to live babies. Then they put the animals into different groups—such as the **mammal** group—that have traits in common. Paleontologists do the same thing with fossils.

Until the 1970s, scientists grouped animals using a method invented by Carolus Linnaeus almost 300 years earlier. For the most part, it was a good method—but it grouped animals based on what they had in common *and* on what they did not. Even if one species had many traits in common with another species, a few differences could keep them from being part of the same group.

*Mammals were alive throughout the Age of Dinosaurs. Here, the dinos* Ornithomimus *tries to pull the mammal* Didelphodon *from its burrow.*

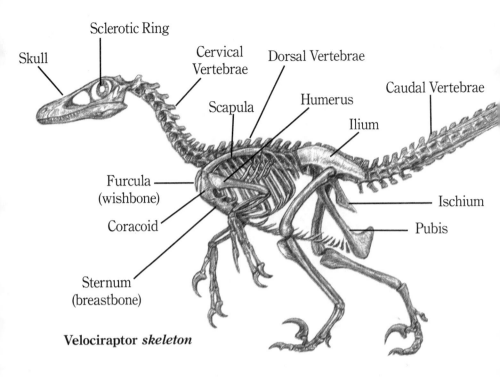

Sclerotic Ring

Skull

Cervical Vertebrae

Dorsal Vertebrae

Caudal Vertebrae

Scapula

Humerus

Ilium

Furcula (wishbone)

Coracoid

Ischium

Pubis

Sternum (breastbone)

**Velociraptor** *skeleton*

Paleontologists knew that modern birds and dinosaurs had *some* things in common. But in general, they seemed more different than the same.

Then in the 1960s, a paleontologist named John Ostrom began to study and compare the bones of the raptor *Deinonychus* with the bones of modern birds. He found that these two animals were *not* so different after all. In fact, Ostrom's work showed that their bones had twenty-two traits in common.

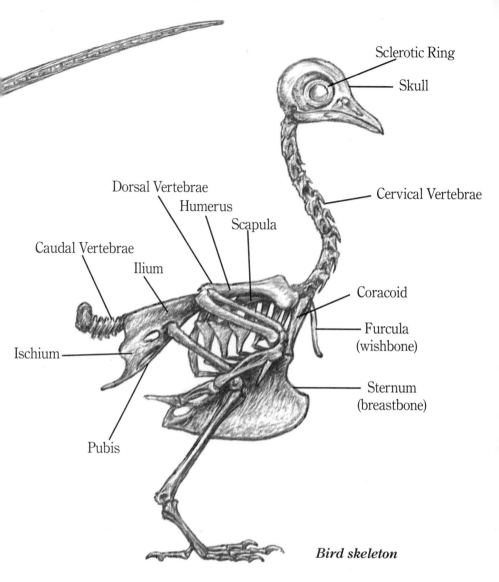

Sclerotic Ring

Skull

Cervical Vertebrae

Dorsal Vertebrae

Humerus

Scapula

Caudal Vertebrae

Ilium

Coracoid

Ischium

Furcula
(wishbone)

Sternum
(breastbone)

Pubis

*Bird skeleton*

Ostrom had the same idea as Huxley had, almost a hundred years before. Modern birds *must* be closely related to theropod dinosaurs! Other paleontologists had felt this way, but Ostrom's work finally made the idea more accepted.

At around this time, scientist Willi Hennig developed a new method of putting animals into groups. Hennig's method was called **cladistics**. It was different from the Linnaean method. Cladistics grouped animals based *just* on traits they had in common.

Hennig decided that the best way to find out which extinct species were the relatives of modern species was to follow common traits through the **fossil record**. (This is everything we know about the past based on all the fossils so far collected.) For example, claws that can be drawn back are a common trait in both extinct and modern cats.

Hennig knew that evolution caused even closely related species to develop *some* different traits. He realized that even if two groups of animals seemed very different (for example, lions and tigers) but shared traits that no other group had, then the two must be related.

By the early 1980s, a paleontologist named Jacques Gauthier had compared the fossils of *Archaeopteryx,* other ancient birds, and different theropods with the bones of modern birds. The groups had so many traits in common that Gauthier felt birds were not *cousins* of dinosaurs. Cladistics showed they *were* dinosaurs that had never become extinct!

Archaeopteryx

*Hey, a turkey is no* T. rex! *I'd like to see some of these "common traits" myself.*

A good idea. Let's do just that.

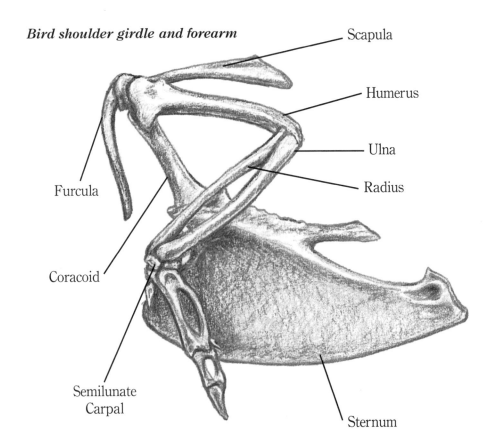

*Bird shoulder girdle and forearm*

Scapula

Humerus

Ulna

Radius

Furcula

Coracoid

Semilunate
Carpal

Sternum

# Chapter 5
# Head, Shoulders, Knees, and Toes

When Gauthier said that birds were
dinosaurs, he *really* meant it! Think of birds
and raptors as if they were house cats and
tigers. Even though these two animals are
very different, they are still both cats.
Paleontologists have discovered twenty-

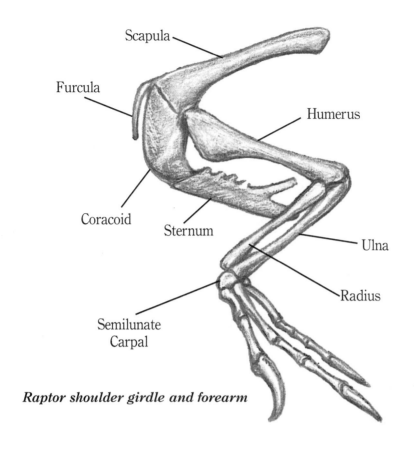

*Raptor shoulder girdle and forearm*

three traits shared by birds and their closest relatives in the raptor group.

For example, raptors had long arms with long, thin hands and fingers. The bones in their arms and hands were much like the bones in a bird's wings. Other bones in their upper bodies show that raptors had the same kind of muscles to move their arms that birds use to fly.

In fact, when raptors grasped at their prey, they probably moved their arms the way birds flap their wings. The motion of a bird's wings while flying is called the **flight stroke**. Paleontologists believe that the flight stroke evolved from the way raptors moved their arms—just as raptors evolved this movement from *their* relatives.

Another trait that modern birds and most theropods share is called the **furcula**. That's another name for the wishbone in a bird's chest. Finding the furcula in raptors was important because it is a very special feature. For a long time, paleontologists thought that only birds had it. Now the fossil record shows that the furcula evolved in theropods—before birds even existed!

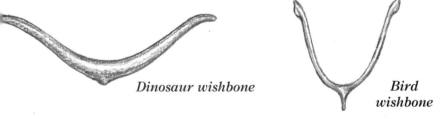

*Dinosaur wishbone*              *Bird wishbone*

The **pubis** bone in raptors is also very much like the pubis bone in modern birds. In the raptor, this bone withstood the shock of the dinosaur leaping onto its prey. Later, this bone would help modern birds withstand the impact of landing from flight.

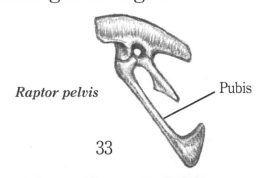

*Raptor pelvis*              Pubis

Birds and raptors also have large heads compared to their small bodies. A large head means a large brain. And a large brain means a smarter animal. Smarter animals are better able to hunt, run, and control the muscles of the flight stroke.

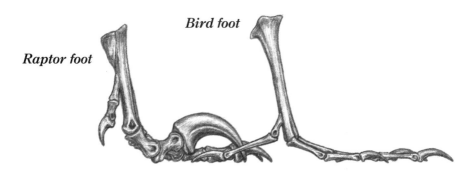

*Bird foot*

*Raptor foot*

Even though the feet and toes of a raptor look different from those of a bird, many of the bones are almost the same. If you look at the foot of *Archaeopteryx,* you can almost see the "step" between a raptor's foot and a modern bird's.

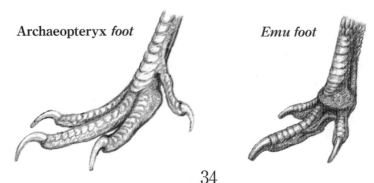

Archaeopteryx *foot*

*Emu foot*

Modern birds have hollow bones, and the fossils of raptors and their relatives show that they had hollow bones, too. Even big theropods, like *Tyrannosaurus,* had them. Solid bones are hard, but very heavy. Hollow bones are sturdy, but lightweight. Lighter bones allowed theropods to run faster. In modern birds, it means they have less weight to carry when flying.

**Theropod bone (hollow)**

*Okay. So birds and raptors have a lot of traits in common. It still seems like a big jump from having traits in common to flying around like birds.*

You are right. That is *just* what took place—a big jump! (More or less.)

# Chapter 6
# From Feathers to Flight

It's important to remember that evolution takes place over long, long periods of time. The traits found in raptors and birds originally evolved in *their* relatives. The evolution of feathers happened in much the same way. The first feathers did not just "show up" on an animal. They were not like the feathers of modern birds. They were much more like hairs, or the wispy feathers of a modern emu. These feathers were not good for flying. Paleontologists think that they were for warmth. (If the weather was getting cooler, then dinosaurs with feathers were likely to stay warmer. Their chances for survival increased, just as the chances of survival *decreased* for dinosaurs without feathers.)

*Emu feather*

Nomingia, *a bizarre feathered dinosaur from Asia*

This new feature was useful to the theropods who had it. As their feathers became more developed, the surface area of their arms increased. (That means that feathers made their arms wider and flatter.) This helped them run faster by pushing more air as they moved their arms. (Think of how fins help you swim faster.) It also caused the theropods to stay in the air a little longer each time they leapt. And that helped them leap farther when they jumped off a high rock or tree limb.

All these traits worked together to help the theropods stay alive. John Ostrom had an idea about how this led to them taking flight.

Over millions of years, a group of theropods developed many bird-like traits. Ostrom imagined them running after flying insects. Their arms moved in the flight stroke as they ran and grasped at their prey. Those who could leap higher and stay in the air longer were better hunters. This made them more likely to stay alive and to have babies. Eventually, their arms became enough like wings to make bursts of actual flight!

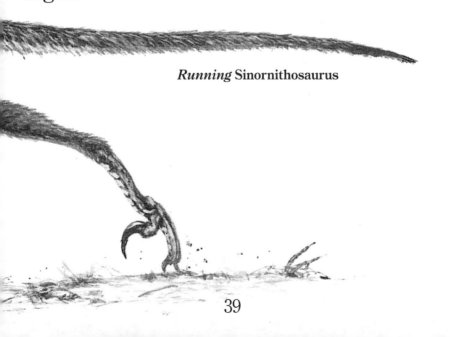

*Running* Sinornithosaurus

Paleontologists do not think that these early bird relatives were good fliers. They could probably stay in the air for only a few moments, like a chicken. But being able to fly—even briefly—was a useful trait. It would allow the bird relatives to travel farther in search of prey, and to catch prey more easily. It would also help them avoid predators.

Over millions of years, these early flying dinosaurs evolved into species such as *Archaeopteryx*. In turn, *Archaeopteryx*—or an animal like it—evolved into the thousands of species of birds that exist today!

irds continued to evolve through the Age of Dinosaurs to the present.
ere some Late Cretaceous birds stand on the back of their distant

Pteranodon

Hesperornis

# Chapter 7
# Dinosaurs Alive!

Those early birds were not the only animals to have evolved the power of flight. Early insects buzzed through the air long before flying **reptiles** such as *Pteranodon* (tuh-RAN-uh-don). Bats are mammals that also took to the air. And there are extinct **prehistoric** birds, such as *Hesperornis* (hes-per-OR-nis), that lost the ability to fly, much like the modern ostrich.

Paleontologists have not found fossils for *all* of the species connecting dinosaurs to birds. The tiny bones of these small animals do not fossilize as easily as big bones. Scientists have to look at the fossils they do have and make educated guesses about the ones they do not have.

Still, there is enough fossil **evidence** today to show that birds are the direct descendants (like *really* great-grandchildren) of small meat-eating theropods. Birds are dinosaurs just as much as *Tyrannosaurus rex, Triceratops,* and *Brachiosaurus* are dinosaurs! So until paleontologists find a fossil that proves them wrong, you can point to the smallest sparrow at a bird feeder and say *dinosaurs are alive!*

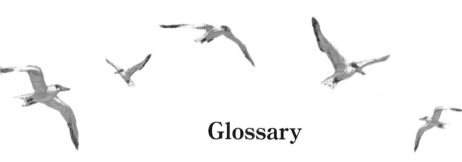

# Glossary

**Cladistics:** A method of grouping animals based on special traits they have in common.

**Descendant:** A person or animal that is the offspring of a specific relative. For example, a child is a descendant of its parents.

**Environment:** All the conditions surrounding a living thing at a given time.

**Evidence:** Proof of something.

**Evolution:** The development of plants and animals since the formation of Earth.

**Extinct:** No longer existing.

**Fossil:** A trace of past life found in rock.

**Furcula:** The wishbone.

**Mammal:** A warm-blooded animal that has fur or hair and whose babies are fed with milk from their mother's breast.

**Natural selection:** The process by which animals better suited to their environment survive and have babies.

**Predator:** An animal that hunts other animals for food.

**Prehistoric:** Before written history.

**Prey:** An animal hunted for food.

**Pubis:** A bone found in the pelvis, or lower trunk of the body.

**Raptor:** An informal term used to describe dromaeosaurs, or raptor dinosaurs.

**Reptile:** A crocodile, snake, lizard, turtle, or one of their closest relatives (such as pterosaurs and dinosaurs).

**Species:** A group of animals that can breed with each other and produce fertile offspring.

**Theropod:** A member of a group of two-legged, mostly meat-eating dinosaurs.

**Trait:** An inherited feature, like being able to lay eggs or to fly.